LASTING LETTERS

The dedication of the slate on 21st November 1979

LASTING LETTERS

EDITED BY
ROSAMOND McKITTERICK
&
LIDA LOPES CARDOZO

CAMBRIDGE
CARDOZO KINDERSLEY EDITIONS
1992

CARDOZO KINDERSLEY EDITIONS
NUMBER EIGHT

Copyright © 1992
Rosamond McKitterick & Lida Lopes Cardozo

First Edition 1992
Published by
Cardozo Kindersley Editions
152 Victoria Road
Cambridge CB4 3DZ

British Library Cataloguing in Publication Data
McKitterick, Rosamond

Lasting Letters

ISBN 1 874426 02 3 HB
ISBN 1 874426 03 1 PB

Designed by Lida Lopes Cardozo & Rosamond McKitterick
Typeset by Goodfellow & Egan, Cambridge in Monotype
Octavian, designed by David Kindersley & Will Carter
Printed by BAS Printers, Over Wallop, Hants.

We need a bigger picture of mediæval life.
It was slow and matched our brains,
our sight and our legs.
It went on around us.
We had time to improve with the help of
religion.
We must not forget, when writing about
this period, the huge growth of monasteries
and their buildings. Never surpassed.
WHY!
Everything grew out of experience, little
bit by little bit. We can no longer do it.
It was all done by many people.
Things were loved;
Things were made to last, and did so.
They were not abandoned because of
fashion. This has gone!
It is definitely no help to talk about a
non-mechanised age.
Before this dreadful irreligious age we
were able to think & do & make & improve.

HEAVEN was once in reach.
HELL is not now far away.

Written by David Kindersley as a guide for this book

HERE
REST THE MORTAL REMAINS ⒠ ABBOTS FROM 1077 To 1401

· PAUL OF CAEN ·
RICHARD d'ALBINI
GEoFFReY ⒠ GoRRoN
· RALPH GUBION ·
ROBERT of GORRON
· SIMON ·
WARIN ⒠ CAMBRiDGE
· JOHN de CELLA ·
WILLIAM
OF TRUMPINGToN
JOHN ⒠ HERTFORD
JOHN de la MOOTE

And also of
RoBERT of the CHAMBeR
father of Pope Adrian IV
ADAM the CELARER
Prior ADAM WiTTeNHAM
ADAM ROUS
Surgeon to Edward III

REMOVED in 1978 from
The CHAPTER HOUSE

SEEK FIRST THE KINGDOM OF GOD

The original intention for this book was to describe how the slate commemorating the abbots of St Albans was designed and cut. After David had written his account, it became apparent to us that without an explanation of how the abbots came to be reinterred under the slate, and without some knowledge of who they were and what they had achieved, a description of the work on the slate would not be enough to celebrate the abbots, the slate and the tradition they both embody.

This is where Rosamond pointed out that these were the very men who had presided over the most glorious period of book production of St Albans and who were vitally concerned with letter forms and the durability of the written word. Once we had asked the Biddles, Patrick Barry and Robert Runcie to add their sections, David Kindersley's account of the slate had its proper context.

We began work on Lasting Letters in the summer of 1991. Then, on a memorable day just before Christmas, while the children played upstairs, we sat down to decide exactly what we wanted the book to look like and somehow found that we had actually designed it ourselves. Work thereafter was squeezed into long evenings for the rest of the winter. We are especially grateful to all those who have contributed to the making of this book, not least to David and Lucy McKitterick, David, Paul, Hallam and Vincent Kindersley for their loving support.

Lida Lopes Cardozo
Rosamond McKitterick
Cambridge, 15th April
1992

INTRODUCTION

REMOVED in 1978 from
The CHAPTER HOUSE

SEEK FIRST
THE KINGDOM OF
GOD

INTRODUCTION

THE INSPIRATION FOR THIS BOOK
is to be found on an exquisite slab of Welsh
slate, marvellously inscribed by David
Kindersley and Lida Lopes Cardozo above
the presbytery steps and in front of the
high altar of the abbey church of St Albans.
The words in Roman capitals are cut with
artistry and artifice. They record the
names of sixteen 'Fathers of the Abbey'
whose bones now lie beneath the floor of
the high altar sanctuary. The inscription is
laid out in a long and narrow column; but
each line of letters decreases slightly in size
as you read down the inscription. Seen by
the celebrant standing at the altar, their
prominence gradually yields to the
mystery of the sacrament he is to receive.
Seen by the communicant making his way
to the altar, all the letters seem to be of the
same size and are equally legible.

*in front of the
High Altar*

*gradually yields
to the mystery*

The bones of the abbots were recovered
from a lovingly skilled excavation of the
ancient chapter house. They were reverently
reburied beneath the sanctuary and the great
memorial was unveiled. None of us who
took part in that service on November 21st
1979 will ever forget the sense of unity
within the love of God. We were bilingual
again, mingling French and English. The
monks of Bec and the Benedictines of
England rendered the evening office of
Vespers in Latin, the congregation was led

*the sense of
unity*

11

by 'our Cardinal' and 'our Bishop'. We seemed to be emancipated from the warfare of the centuries, and the petty irritations of contemporary rivalry.

Behold how good and joyful a thing it is Brethren to dwell together in unity.

The words of T S Eliot come to mind:

This is the use of memory:
For liberation — not less of love but expanding
Of love beyond desire, and so liberation
From the future as well as the past.

In the timeless continuities of Christian pilgrimage we were aware of the presence of God which was not to be grasped, manipulated, contrived, but to be quietly and steadily received.

In the past decade I have seen the resurrection of a new chapter house for our own day. The song school, the refectory, the study centre and the counselling rooms, all these are equipping us for the ancient ministry of worship, welcome, learning, and charity.

I dare to think that it all has something to do with that slate and the story told in these pages. Spacing and balance and perspective of the words have a simplicity and vigour born of discipline but revealed in natural grace. So it is with the disciple. There should be no doubt about the discipline but what should be obvious is the simplicity and the grace.

a simplicity and vigour born of discipline

Those who speak to us of faith most movingly across the ages have not hesitated to compare the spiritual with the artistic insight. These are both related to the roots of our civilisation and the hope of all our futures. 'Seek first the kingdom of God' is the bold proclamation on the stone which lists the abbots who lead us towards the holy mysteries. It is God whom Augustine described as *Pulchritudo tam antiqua tam nova:* 'Beauty ever old and ever new'.

compare the spiritual with the artistic insight

13

EXCAVATION

HERE

REST THE MORTAL REMAINS ⓕ ABBOTs FROM 1077 To 1401

EXCAVATiON

THE DISCOVERY OF THE MEDIAEVAL
CHAPTER HOUSE AND THE
IDENTIFICATION OF THE BURIALS
OF THE ABBOTS OF ST ALBANS.

Within twelve days of the dissolution of the
Abbey of St Albans in December 1539 the
sacred vessels and treasures of the shrine
were removed to London for the king's use.
Within as many years the abbey's great
treasure of buildings was as thoroughly
destroyed. Of the whole vast complex
covering the hill south of the abbey church,
grouped around the cloister and half a
dozen other courts, the agglomeration of
twelve centuries, only the gate house
survived intact. The church became a
parish church, the retrochoir and lady
chapel were severed from the rest by a
public right of way, and walled off to
become the setting of the refounded school.

    The second half of the nineteenth
century saw the repair and reconstruction
of the abbey church, by then sadly
decayed, as the centre of the new diocese of
St Albans, founded in 1877. From the start,
all the functions of a cathedral church had
to be housed within the one structure:
vestries, song school, libraries, meeting
rooms, and offices. Within a century the
situation had become intolerable. In the
early 1970s the Dean and Cathedral
Council began the search for a solution.

dissolution

*the abbey's
great treasure of
buildings was as
thoroughly
destroyed*

*reconstruction of
the abbey
church*

*the situation
had become
intolerable*

17

Deprived of all the great buildings which
had served the mediaeval abbey, they

a new building   decided that only a new building could

St Albans Abbey with
David Kindersley and
the Dean of St Albans.
The new chapter house
on the right, now
stands where the
abbots were originally
buried.

solve the problem and that the only
suitable and practicable site was that
occupied centuries before by the chapter
house. This lay immediately south of the
abbey church and by the 1970s was
occupied by a path, the deanery drive, and
part of the deanery garden. After a period
of uncertainty which included a lengthy
public enquiry the necessary consents were
obtained, with the proviso that there should

St Albans Abbey,
looking down from the
roof of the south
transept at Robert of
Gorron's chapter
house

archaeological excavation

first be an archaeological excavation to record all that survived of the mediaeval chapter house and adjacent structures. This excavation took place over ten weeks in the summer – one of the wettest in recent years – of 1978.

a vast chapter house

Within a few weeks the outline of a vast rectangular chapter house had been uncovered, over 91 feet long and 29 feet wide internally, almost exactly the same size as the chapter house of Canterbury Cathedral, which still survives. The south wall had been mostly robbed away for reuse of its stone, but enough remained of

the building was twelfth century in date

the other three walls to show that the building was twelfth century in date: it must in fact be the chapter house built by Abbot Robert of Gorron 'from the foundations' at some time between 1154 and 1166. Six deep buttresses added against the outside walls showed that it

reconstructed late in the Middle Ages

had been reconstructed late in the Middle Ages, presumably as a result of the works of Abbot John of Whethamstede in his second abbacy [1452–65], completed by Abbot William of Wallingford [1476–92] at a cost of a thousand pounds.

This sum is so large that Whethamstede and Wallingford must virtually have rebuilt the chapter house. Indeed we know from

study of the carved stones

study of the carved stones recovered in the excavation that they created a stone vault and new windows which will have made the chapter house one of the grandest rooms in late mediaeval England. Nevertheless, they left the plan unchanged and the lower part of the Norman walls, below window level, in position. They also left untouched along the walls the stone benches on which the monks sat in chapter and the magnificent floor of glazed tiles decorated in relief, forming in its patterns and walkways a carpet to the whole. The tiles had been put down by Robert of Gorron in the mid-twelfth century and so had been in continuous use for four and a half centuries when the chapter house was demolished following the dissolution in 1539.

the magnificent floor of glazed tiles

Although the tiles had been badly damaged and only about a fifth of them remained in position, it was possible to see in the floor

fourteen graves

the outlines of fourteen graves, most of which lay along the axis of the chapter house from the west door eastward. The abbot's seat would have been in the centre of the east end, flanked by the great officers of the house – prior, sacrist, cellarer, hordarian, pitancer, forester, and others. We may thus imagine the abbot in chapter looking down the centre of the floor at the burial places of his predecessors, for we know, as we shall see, that these were the graves of former abbots. They were all once marked by marble slabs, set into the tiled floor and carved with their images and epitaphs. In the middle of the floor, interrupting the line of graves, stood the lectern from which each day of the year a chapter of the Rule was read, hence 'chapter house'.

marked by
marble slabs

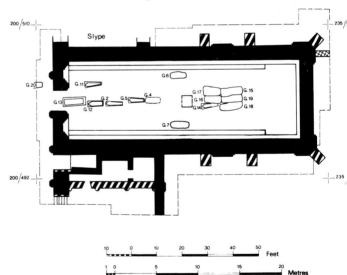

The internal reconstruction of the dorter undercroft by John de la Moote as abbot (1396–1401), and the reconstruction of the chapter house by Abbots Whethamstede (1452–1465) and Wallingford (1476–1492) showing the position of the abbots' graves

We can identify the graves because they were recorded when still visible in the early fifteenth century. The original account is in Latin. Here the names are given in a standard form and dates have been added in brackets.

"After the Conquest the bodies of the abbots were buried in the chapter house. At the door lies Abbot John de la Moote [d.1401] under a flat marble stone decorated with his effigy in the middle and an epitaph. Next, that is towards the east end of the chapter house, the bodies of four abbots lie one after another under marble slabs engraved with their images and epitaphs: Abbot Warin of Cambridge [d.1195], Abbot Ralph Gobion [d.1151], Abbot William of Trumpington [d.1235], and Abbot John of Hertford [d.1265], all of whose praises and deserts are carried to the stars of the firmament.

On the east side of the lectern lie the bodies of six abbots buried there one after another, namely: Abbot Paul of Caen [d.1093], who was a Norman, Richard d'Albini [d.1119], a Norman, Geoffrey of Gorron [d.1146], also a Norman, and Abbot Robert of Gorron [d.1166], Simon [d.1183], and John de Cella [d.1214]. They rest under marble slabs bearing their epitaphs appropriately set down, and their praises and good deeds have merited the Kingdom of Heaven.

About the middle of the chapter house on the south side lies Adam Wittenham [d. before 1396], formerly cellarer, forester,

We can identify the graves

the bodies of six abbots

23

John de la Moote lying
in his grave

and prior of this monastery. On the opposite side lies Master Adam Rous [d.1379], at one time surgeon to King Edward III. On the same side [that is the north], near the door of the chapter house, lies Dom Adam the Cellarer [d. about 1180], inappropriately called 'Lyons'. He rests under a marble slab with keys engraved on it. The old stone, which projected above the pavement and was therefore an inconvenience to those passing by, was removed and put to one side. Bits used once to be chipped off it, powdered, and drunk when needed as a cure for various diseases."

a marble slab with keys engraved on it

The burials listed in this late mediaeval account correspond precisely in number and position to the graves visible in the wrecked floor of the chapter house as first uncovered in 1978. The marble slabs had gone, removed at the dissolution, and the graves of the abbots, except that of John de la Moote, had all been ransacked and their bones disturbed and sometimes scattered. But enough remained to show the location of the graves and to enable the bones to be gathered together and in some cases at least attributed to individual burials, which were later the subject of intensive forensic investigation.

all been ransacked

the subject of intensive forensic investigation

The burial of John of Hertford in 1265 was the last in a line of ten Norman and later abbots laid to rest in the Chapter House. With the one exception of John de la Moote, buried at the door of the chapter

25

Adam the Cellarer
lying in his grave

house in 1401, all the abbots after this were buried in the presbytery, before or beside the high altar of the abbey church.

Fourteen graves had been expected and fourteen were found when the floor was uncovered. When the floor was taken up two earlier chapter houses were discovered and in them two earlier graves. Both these earlier chapter houses had apsidal east ends, unlike the great building of Robert of Gorron which was square-ended. In the apse of the older and smaller of the earlier structures, there was a large empty burial pit. It seems certain that this was the

The building of St Albans Abbey in the reign of King Offa of Mercia in the eighth century. Dublin, Trinity College MS 177, folio 60 recto

27

burial place of Paul of Caen

original burial place of Paul of Caen, builder of the Norman abbey and of this, the earliest of the chapter houses. When the chapter house was for the second time rebuilt and extended between 1154 and 1166, Paul's body was translated to its final resting place further east, before the abbot's seat.

Adam the Cellarer

Immediately south of the grave of Adam the Cellarer, below the tiled floor which here survived intact, lay an earlier and deeper grave. This had been concealed by the tiles and was unknown to the writer of the late mediaeval account, or at least unmentioned because invisible. Its presence was not entirely unexpected, however. The abbey's chronicle, The *Deeds of the Abbots*, records that Robert of the Chamber, father of Nicholas Breakspear, Pope Adrian IV [1154–9], had been buried in the chapter house, not far from the grave of Abbot Richard [d'Albini, 1097–1119], 'his own merits and those of his son, the Lord Pope, compelling it', and that his grave had afterwards been covered by the paving tiles.

Robert of the Chamber

This notice of Robert's burial must go back to the time of the second chapter house, rebuilt and extended for the first time in the earlier twelfth century. When Richard d'Albini died in 1119 his grave can only have been placed within the first or second chapter house, for the position it finally occupied in the third chapter house was not within the building at the

Richard d'Albini

time of his death. Richard's body must therefore have been translated eastward to this final position during or after the rebuilding by Robert of Gorron between 1154 and 1166.

The identification of Robert of the Chamber's grave rests on several considerations: it is the only grave not otherwise accounted for within the chapter house; it is the only grave covered by the tiles of the floor; it lies, not adjacent to the final position of the grave of Abbot Richard, where there is no unidentified burial, but adjacent to one of the two possible original positions of Richard's grave; unlike the burials of the abbots it

it is the only grave covered by tiles

29

lies to one side of the axis; and at the time of burial it was the only grave in the chapter house *of a person of less than abbatial rank*.

Robert's grave contained the body of an elderly man accompanied by a decayed pewter chalice resting on the right side of his chest, demonstrating that he was a priest. This is a point of more than usual interest for it was one of the Emperor Frederick Barbarossa's complaints against Pope Adrian that he was the son of a priest. This may be true, but only in the sense that Robert probably became a priest after separating from his wife on grounds of religion and entering the house of St Albans as a monk.

of a person of less than abbatial rank

The mortal remains of John de la Moote, Warin of Cambridge and Adam the Cellarer ready for reburial

The slate being placed
in position

On completion of the excavation in 1978, the bones of the abbots and others buried in the chapter house were minutely examined by Dr Michael Donmall to establish where possible the age at death and physical condition of the persons represented. The bones were then placed, as far as possible body by body, in stout plastic bags labelled inside and out with plastic tags giving the archaeological field references and personal identifications. The

the bones of the abbots

body by body, in stout plastic bags

31

*placed in
specially made
lead boxes*

bags themselves were placed in specially made lead boxes.

When the time came in 1979 the boxes were placed in a brick-lined grave specially prepared at the head of the steps before the high altar of the abbey church. Here they were covered with a great slate bearing the names and titles of those who had once lain in the chapter house.

*covered with a
great slate*

The abbots who ruled the monastery of St Albans from 1077 to 1265 and from 1396 to 1401 thus came to rest among their successors before the high altar, covered as in the places of their first resting with a monument appropriate to the memory of those who in their day had 'merited the Kingdom of God'.

SUCCESSION

PAUL OF CAEN
RICHARD d'ALBINI
GEOFFREY O GORRON
RALPH GUBION
ROBERT OF GORRON
SIMON
WARIN O CAMBRIDGE
JOHN de CELLA
WILLIAM
OF TRUMPINGTON
JOHN O HERTFORD
JOHN de la MOOTE

ROSAMOND McKITTERICK

lꝰ amās de
um. uel ama
tuſ a deo. Qui
dm̄ amat ut'
a deo uult ama
ri. ad se putet
euangelium
ſcribi. ꝛ ut bo
num depoſi
tum: ſibi com
mendari.

=to enī: mul
theopi
ta p̃terit: que
aliī dicunt' ut
le. ut eo
diuerſa in euan
gelio gr̄a re ſiul
gnoſcaſ
geret. ꝛ p̃priiſ
eo̅ uerbo
quibuſdā: ſin
guli libri: myſterio
rum geſtorumꝗ miraculiſ emineret.

rum de quibꝯ eru
ditus eſ: uerita
tem.

vnde ꝛ a
paulo lau
dat̅ ꝗ̄
omnia aſ
ſecutuſ e̅.
nō quod
omn̄a ſcri
pſerit: ꝗ̄
nec mundus capit......

 m̄ poſt me
etiā te piſca
torem homi
num. Mini
rat'. quando
tollit cruce̅
ſequitur....

C E rudit' eſ. Hon noua
theophilo p̃mittūt' ſ; ea
de quibꝯ e̅ eruditꝯ. ut ꝗ̄ qd
ordine̅. de dr̄o ut' a dr̄o ge
ſtum dictū ne ſit: agnoſcat
Quia p̃ſect'? n̄ ſolū in in̄m̄
credere. ſ; ꝛ fidem p̃ptie
diuinitatiſ ꝛ tēm pan ecꝰ diſpen
ſationiſ illi: debet ordine̅ noſſe.

in diebuſ herodiſ
gena regnat...

regiſ iudee
ſacerdos
quidam

¶ſam̄: alienī
acer
doſ qui
dam. Do
cer diui

Jacobꝯ
Fuit
in die
buſ ui
tuluſ:
ſacerdo
taliſ ho
ſtia. p̃
uituliſ
g̅: hoc
euange
luum
figura
tur. in
quo. a
ſacerdotibꝯ incho
atur. ꝛ in uitulo
conſummatur.
xp̄o. ꝗ̄r. v mun

Jm
pleuit
ordinem
dirit re
gem. re
gionem
in qua
fuit. ſa
cerdote̅
ꝛ gēnt
euſ. ꝛ ꝗ̄r
orem il
luſ in
dicat...

SUCCESSION

St Albans Abbey is built on one of the
oldest Christian sites in England, with an
unbroken tradition of Christian worship
and devotion. On the hill outside the
Roman city of Verulamium, Alban was
martyred for his faith in about A.D. 209.
Thereafter, Alban was remembered and
revered. Bede, in his *Historia ecclesiastica
gentis anglorum*, described the church of
'wonderful workmanship' built on St
Albans hill, 'when peaceful Christian times
returned', to honour the saint.

As well as the church, a monastery
appears to have been founded there as
early as the reign of King Offa of Mercia
[d.796]. Although little is known of this
Anglo-Saxon monastery at St Albans, and
the earliest charters purporting to record
gifts of land made to it in the eighth
century are thought to be spurious, it
seems clear that the abbey played an
important role in the religious life of
southern England, at least in the late
Anglo-Saxon period. It enjoyed royal
patronage, and in the tenth century was
one of the monasteries to which the
Benedictine Rule was introduced by
Oswald of Worcester [d.992], one of the
great reforming bishops, who placed
Aelfric, later Archbishop of Canterbury
[995-1005], at St Albans as abbot. Records
survive of many rich estates granted to the

*Alban was
martyred for his
faith*

*Anglo-Saxon
monastery at St
Albans*

*it enjoyed royal
patronage*

(opposite)
A glossed Gospel Book
written at St Albans
Abbey in early Gothic
script at the end of the
twelfth century, that
is, under Warin of
Cambridge. This
shows the first chapter
of St Luke. Cambridge,
Trinity College MS
B.5.3, folio 111 verso

35

abbey, by the king, by bishops and by the laity both before and after the Norman Conquest. The spiritual reputation of St Albans as well as its material wealth, indeed, appear to have made it represent something of a prize in Norman eyes after the Conquest, for it was Paul of Caen [1077-1093], a nephew of Archbishop Lanfranc of Canterbury, who was installed as the first abbot under Norman rule in 1077.

spiritual reputation and material wealth

For the material wealth it received, in exchange the monastery offered prayers for the souls of the donors. With its material welfare increased, its spiritual power was enhanced. Without the material base afforded by the gifts of pious laymen and laywomen, and by bishops and bequests from clerics, and, above all, new recruits for the religious community from the lay population, the monastery could not have survived. The ties of kinship, land and gratitude anchored the monastery within the community. Further, the monastery ministered to the religious needs of the surrounding population; it provided an essential link with the holy, a visible contact with God and his saints, a focus for religious loyalties and devotion and for service to the cult of the local saint, Alban. All joined, therefore, at whatever level they could manage, in the devotion to God and to the saint who had died for his faith.

anchored the monastery within the community

St Albans' debt to its Anglo-Saxon founders is clear. Not only was the Rule of

St Benedict followed as the custom of the house, the lands and cloistral buildings essential for the maintenance of the monks adding to the abbot's property, but liturgical observance, the pursuit of learning and the production of books were established as an essential part of the monastic life. The Norman abbots and monks built on these foundations. While no evidence survives of an original scriptorium at St Albans before the Conquest, there are traces of pre-Conquest books at the abbey among the later manuscripts. A manuscript written in the time of Abbot Paul of Caen, for example, contains pre-Norman liturgical and hagiographical material, including a Life of the tenth century reformer Dunstan, archbishop of Canterbury [d.988], and is written in a markedly English caroline minuscule hand. English scribes in pre-

the pursuit of learning

The beginning of the Rule of St Benedict. The manuscript was written in Anglo-Saxon square minuscule script in the mid-tenth century at St Augustine's Canterbury. Cambridge, Trinity College MS O.2.30, folio 130 recto

Conquest England had developed their own distinctive 'insular' script from the Old Roman script system. Even when the Continental script type of caroline minuscule was introduced into England in *English scribes* the tenth century, the English scribes included some of their own peculiar insular letter forms. That at least one English scribe can be observed among the earliest manuscripts from post-Conquest St Albans indicates that some English monks may have remained in the abbey under the new Norman abbot and were able to transmit their English methods of script formation and book production to their Norman brother monks who, in their turn, introduced the early Gothic script and *French methods of book production.

French methods of book production

It is, however, only under the Norman abbots that St Albans' prominence in England can be fully documented. In its marvellous buildings, its liturgical observance, its encouragement of learning, its fervent spiritual life and, above all, in the books they produced, the St Albans' monks have left us a record of their lofty cultural and spiritual standing among other English and Continental Benedictine houses of the twelfth and thirteenth centuries. St Albans, for example, *a grammar school* maintained a grammar school until the end of the twelfth century, headed by *magistri* who had been trained in the Continental schools of St Victor in Paris and of Salerno. With the other English monasteries,

Hugh of St Victor teaching three monastic pupils in Paris. The book was written and decorated at St Albans at the end of the twelfth century. Oxford, Bodleian MS Laud misc. 409, folio 3 verso

St Albans dominated education and learning in England until the end of the twelfth century. They were the principal disseminators and preservers of learning and knowledge through their libraries and their book production.
The manuscripts produced by St Albans

39

shed light on the abbey's history, its intellectual contacts, and the vital contribution made by each abbot to the work of the scriptorium in the twelfth and thirteenth centuries. Those abbots, whose graves and mortal remains under the chapter house first built by Paul of Caen and rebuilt by Robert of Gorron, were rediscovered in the excavation of 1978 conducted by Martin Biddle and Birthe Kjølbye-Biddle, and who were reinterred under David Kindersley's magnificent slate in 1979, are also the abbots who put much of their energy into the creation of the abbey buildings and the promotion of the work of the scriptorium.

intellectual contacts

Paul of Caen, for example, presided over the rebuilding of the Anglo-Saxon abbey church and monastic buildings, and had the inspired idea of reusing Roman bricks from the city of Verulamium for the work. He worked to acquire and retrieve lands, and tithes, and it is an indication of the prosperity of the abbey under his rule that he was able to set up a number of dependent cells at Wallingford, Tynemouth, Belvoir, Hertford and Binham. Subsequent abbots followed Paul's lead in providing both support for the scriptorium, augmenting the abbey's wealth, with four more dependent cells being added in the twelfth century, and increasing and embellishing the monastic buildings. Monks from St Albans were elevated to high ecclesiastical positions as bishops and

rebuilding of the Anglo-Saxon abbey

Monks from St Albans became bishops and abbots elsewhere

abbots elsewhere. Thus, quite apart from his securing of privileges and exemptions from episcopal jurisdiction from the Pope in Rome, which enabled St Albans to attain the premier rank among English abbeys, Robert of Gorron [1151-66] rebuilt Paul of Caen's chapter house to accommodate the larger number of monks now at the abbey. From the provision of seating in the new chapter house it can be calculated that there were about ninety monks in the community in the mid-twelfth century. Robert laid out a marvellous glazed and patterned tile floor and translated the bodies of his predecessors, Geoffrey of Gorron [d.1146] and Richard d'Albini [d.1119] to new tombs. Richard d'Albini had embellished the great abbey church and was celebrated for his rigorous monastic observance. Paul of Caen's grave, as well as that of Robert of the Chamber [d.1154-9], father of the only English Pope Nicholas Breakspear, who took the name of Adrian IV, and that of another early abbot Ralph Gobion [d.1151], on the other hand, were left undisturbed. The chapter house continued to serve as a resting place for several more abbots. Robert of Gorron was himself buried there in 1166 at the feet of Paul of Caen, and his successors Simon [d.1183], Warin of Cambridge [d.1195], and John de Cella [d.1214], another great builder who reconstructed the cloister range south of the chapter house, were also buried there.

the new chapter house

rigorous monastic observance

a resting place for several more abbots

William of Trumpington [d.1235] and John of Hertford [d.1273] were the last of the long succession of abbots laid to rest under the chapter house floor. For the most part abbots and important figures were buried thereafter beneath the floor in the presbytery of the new abbey church, the exceptions being Adam Rous, who had acted as surgeon to King Edward III and presumably retired to the abbey to devote his last years to God, Adam Wittenam, a prior of the abbey in the fourteenth century, and Abbot John de la Moote [d.1401].

A detail of David Kindersley's slate (Adam the Cellarer) showing a ligature of LA

the inscribed slate

All these men are now commemorated in the inscribed slate of great beauty made by David Kindersley. It is highly fitting that these men, who did their utmost to promote the written word and learning in the form of the manuscript books produced in the abbey scriptorium, and whose books ranked among the finest in Europe at the time, should be recalled to our hearts and memories in such a manner, with incised letter forms of a grace and clarity that the St Albans' abbots and their master scribes would have loved, both for their form and for the craftsmanship that created them.

incised letter forms

It was the decades between 1120 and 1160 which saw the great developments in St Albans' book production, whose impetus and high standards were maintained thereafter until 1235. An essential support for the abbey's book production was the patronage of the abbots, especially Paul of Caen, who instituted a fully professional establishment for copying manuscripts at the abbey, with scribes being allotted a daily food allowance for their work and exemplars to be copied being supplied, in the first instance, from Canterbury. The *Gesta Abbatum* of Matthew Paris [d.1259], himself a monk of St Albans in the thirteenth century, attributes not only the establishment of a workshop or scriptorium for the production of books to Paul, but also the donation of a large number of splendid liturgical and library books. Only two manuscripts now survive from Paul's reign. Paul, according to Matthew Paris, was somewhat contemptuous of the Anglo-Saxon cultural traditions he found in the abbey and did his best to expunge them. Yet it should be clear that the eleventh-century church in Normandy owed an immense debt to imported ideas and personnel and it is likely that in the immediate post-Conquest

St Albans book production

a workshop or scriptorium

period the Normans gained far more culturally, intellectually and materially from the English church than they contributed, and thus that the subsequent development of Anglo-Norman culture was based on a dual foundation to far greater an extent than is usually assumed.

A collection of the works of Lawrence of Durham, showing the author. The book was written and decorated at Durham in the late twelfth century. Durham, University Library, Bishop Cosin's Library MS V.III.1, folio 22 verso

scribes and artists

In the St Albans scriptorium between 1100 and 1120, scribes and artists worked together to produce, on the basis of this dual heritage, a distinctive St Albans' 'house style' of script and decoration of great elegance and regularity based on the new Continental early Gothic script. That is, the scribes of the atelier were all trained to write in a particular homogeneous and identifiable style peculiar to this atelier alone, even though the general type of script was one used by scribes all over Europe at the time. This general script type was modified in various ways, in the shape of particular letters, in the use of serifs and *serifs and* flourishes, in the deployment of capitals *flourishes* and alternative letter forms in headings, and in the layout of the text on the page, to produce distinctive 'house styles'. Although within this 'house style' *'house style' of* individual traits are clear enough for the *script* work of particular scribes to be distinguished, personal traits are subordinated to the creation of a distinctive workshop style, just as David Kindersley's workshop now produces a distinctive 'house style' even though each stone carver has his or her own stylistic conception of the letter forms and the creative dynamic of the layout of the text.

There is no library list to enable us to reconstruct the contents of the St Albans library, but there are about sixty-five extant manuscripts surviving from before *extant* the mid-thirteenth century, and the original *manuscripts* library may have numbered as many as three or four hundred volumes by about 1200. The most distinctive books were produced during the reign of Abbot

45

te & statuā cōt̃ faciem tuā. Quē eñi audientis utilirem
no laborando sudare. & alios detrahendo laborare. dole
re iudeos qd̃ calūniandi eis & irridendi xp̃ianos sit
ablata occasio. & ecc̃lie hominies id despicere. immolate
rare undeaduersarii torqueant̃ Qd̃ si uetus eis tantū in
terpretatio placet quę & michi non displicet & nichil
extra recipiendū putant̃ cur ea quę sub astericis ※
& obelis ÷ ut addita sunt ut amputata legunt̃ & non
eligunt̃ Quare danihelem iuxta theodotionis t̃nslatio
nem ecc̃le susceperunt̃ Cur origene mirantur & euse
bium pamphili cunctas editiones similiter disserentes

Aut ꝗ sunt stulticia pꝗm uera dixerint pferre ꝗ falsa st̃ Unde
aut̃ in nouo testam̃to pbare potuerit assūpta testimonia ꝗ inli
bris uetib; ñ habent̃ hec dicim̃ ne omino calūniantib; tacere
uideam̃ Cetū p sc̃e pauli domm̃tione cui uita uirtut;excpli e
& hos libro ꝗs custochie uirgini xp̃i negare ñ potui decreuim̃
dū sp̃s ho regit ars pph̃aru explanationi incube & omissū tã
diu op ꝗdā p liminio repete̅ pserti cū & admirabili seseq; uir
pamachius hoc ide lrīs flagitet & ño ad patā festinantes
mortifero sirenaru cant̃ surda debeam aure t̃nsire Explic pfac

Iosue fili nun tipū dñi ñ solū ingesti uerū etiā t̃ ieronim̃ in librū
& in nomie gestan̄ t̃nsit iordanen. hostiū regna subuertit. di
uidit t̃rā uictou poplo. & psingulas urbe̅ uiculo. monte. flumina
torrente atꝗ; ꝯfinia. ecc̃lie celestisꝗ; ier t̃n spiritalia regna describit.

Incipiunt capitula libri iesunaue

P romittit d̃s iosue dicens. sicut fui cum moyse ero & tecū .II P repa
rari cibaria iubetur poplo. ut t̃nseant iordanen .III F estinant explo
ratores a iosue inih̃iericho .IIII P romittit d̃ñs iosue dicens. hodie incipi
am exaltare te coram omni isr̃l. ut sciant quia sicut fui cum moyse
ita & tecum sum. V I ubente d̃ño siccat̃ e alueus iordanis cunti isr̃l.
VI D uodecim lapides electi deiordanis alueo ob cōmemoratione futuritem
poris. VII I ntroeunte isr̃l terram chanaan territi sunt cuncti reges .VIII
H ec autem causa est scd̃e circucisionis. IX H uc usꝗ comederunt manna.

X O stendit se angelus d̃ñi iosue qui dixit. princeps exercit̃ d̃ñi sum. XI D e
obsidione uel subuersione muri ih̃iericho. XII I npricatio iosue. XIII P re
uaricatio popli. XIIII C onfortat d̃ñs iosue ad preliandum. XV P ertur
batio regum. XVI S imulatio gabaonitaru. XVII C onglobati quinq;
reges contra iosue ascenderunt. tunc imperauit soli & stetit spatium
diei unius. XVIII I uuante d̃ño uincit se ꝗnq; reges cū exercitu suo. XVIIII
Ruben gd̃ & dimidia tribus manasse terram sibi dari postulantes a moyse
XX H i sunt reges terre quos pcussit iosue & filii isr̃l. XXI D iuidere terras
poplis hortatur d̃ñs iosue. XXII P romissum repete chaleb moxtem he

Geoffrey of Gorron [1119-1146], originally from Le Mans, whose scriptorium was dominated by a Master scribe 'A' and his assistants. It is a time described as a 'great leap forward' at St Albans in terms of intellectual and artistic achievement. An example of Master scribe A's work is to be seen in a codex containing the *Antiquities* of Josephus. He was succeeded by Master Scribe 'B' and his group of scribes, who produced, among other manuscripts, a volume of treatises by Ambrose, Jerome and an anonymous early mediaeval author whose works were mistakenly attributed to Augustine. Ralph Gobion [1146-1151] continued the tradition of the abbot's assuming a major responsibility for the scriptorium. Ralph was a scholar of some reputation and a lover of books who had been trained at Lincoln, and had originally been called on by Abbot Richard d'Albini to head the St Albans grammar school in the city before becoming the first English abbot of the post-Conquest era. The high standards of the St Albans scribes were maintained by a third group working under Abbot Simon [1167-83], an Englishman and local boy in that he had been trained at St Albans itself. Simon's mark of ownership is to be seen in such books as a contemporary copy of the twelfth-century scholar John of Salisbury's *Policraticus*, *Entheticus* and *Metalogicon* and Cambridge, Trinity College O.7.13, a copy of Cassiodorus given by him to the

scribe 'A'

scribe 'B'

a lover of books

(opposite)
A Bible written at St Albans Abbey at the end of the twelfth century by one main hand in the style of 'scribe B'. 'Scribe B' himself takes over for the middle portion of this column from where the finger points. Cambridge, Trinity College Library MS B.5.1, folio 47 verso

St Albans library. He also commissioned glossed copies of the Old and New Testaments. The work of all three groups of scribes can be identified among the extant manuscripts. The writing is highly skilled. It is masterly book making, with a superb sense of letter forms, the deployment of different grades of script from decorated initials and capitals to minuscule, and an artist's attention to matters of design and layout. There is a delightful parallel between the layout of the twelfth-century books of St Albans, with its alternation of minuscule script and capitals, and the layout of the inscribed slate commemorating them. This too, introduces lines of minuscule between capitals, and organizes the space in relation to the letters in the total design, particularly in the use of an O containing an F, in a strikingly similar way.

At first the texts copied appear to have been solidly conservative, with a large proportion of the standard patristic works by such authors as Augustine, Jerome and Ambrose. Under the scholarly abbots Robert of Gorron [1151-66], who took his seat at the Council of Tours in 1163 at the head of all the English abbots, Warin [1183-1195], who was prior before his elevation, and who invited no less a scholar than Alexander Nequam to be head of the St Albans school, and John de Cella [1195-1214], who had been born of a humble family on the abbey's estates before

masterly book making

standard patristic works

(opposite)
A glossed Gospel Book written at St Albans Abbey at the end of the twelfth century, showing the text of St Matthew. The gloss is attributed to Anselm of Laon. Cambridge, Trinity College Library MS B.5.3, folio 46 recto

ñ utante
pparabo
las. quibz
ñ itis uita
etiam pos
siu conseq.

dñ ul di filium ñ con-
fessus est.
dissc qm
uis scm ho-
minem com-
paratione
di ñ e bo-
num. Xpe
autem ñ
renuit testi-
moniū lo-
mtatis. s.
magistri
absq; d eo
excludit er-
rorem. dñ
dicat. cñ
purum lo-
minē me
intelligis
cur uocas
me bonū.
cum nemo
sit bonus
nisi ds ut
ex deo?
ru de bono. s; qui facit
qd bonuē.

Nota duas uitas a
domino e expositas. acti-
uam que ptinet ad le-
gem. yñ dixit. Non ho-
micidium facies etc.
Contemplatiuā. que p

Quid
me inter-
gas de bo-
no? Quia
bonum di-
xit magi-
strum. tñ

filium ñ con-
...

Serua.
ille quesi-
erat quid
boni faci-
am. iste
econtra
illi respon-
det. non
disce may
data sed
serua may
data. qa
deus fac-
tor ratio-
nalis na-
ture illū
docuerat.
ostendens
quia bo-
nus ille
non est?
qui que

Ecce
actiua ui-
ta que ad
legem pti-
net. Nota
quod iusti-
cia legis
suo tempo-
re ñ solum
bona terre-
s; uitam
etiam da-
bat?

Beda.
on est
putandus
iste ut qui

Quid me interrogas de bono? Unus est bonus deus. Si autem

Uiam que ducit ad uitam.

uis ad uitam ingre di: serua mandata. Dicit

Temptando.

Quasi ñ legerit ul deus possit iubere con-
traria.

illi. Que? Ihc autem dixit. Non homicidi um facies. non ad ulterabis. ñ facies furtum. ñ falsum te stimonium di ces. honora pa trem tuum et matrem tuā.

Hō puerilis innocentia et castitas.

Non quod facere s; quod facere est.

et diliges proxi mum tuum: sicut teipsum.

Non uicti tuum.

Dicit ei adolescens. Oī a hec custodi ui a iuuentu

Ioh. Mentitur. quia si diligeret pxri-
mum sicut se: ñ et christis cum sua
paupb; dare iuberet.

becoming prior of Wallingford, however, there is also abundant evidence of St Albans' contacts with the Continental schools, with some of the newer glossed texts by masters in the schools of Paris being introduced as well as works by the most famous English and Continental scholars. Abbot William [1214-35] donated a copy of the writings of Hugh and Richard of St Victor to the abbey library. William was, besides, respected as a disciplinarian, and, like many of his predecessors, as a builder, for it was he who directed the work to complete the west front of the church and the building of a supplementary dormitory as well as being connected with the making and donation of books. John of Hertford [d.1263], another Englishman, continued the work of his predecessor William and presented a fine collection of contemporary theological treatises, copied in the St Albans scriptorium, to Hertford priory.

Thus the men who were elected to the abbacy were, without exception, men distinguished for their scholarship and for their patronage of learning. Contacts with some of the famous Continental schools in the second half of the twelfth century, such as St Victor in Paris, gradually transformed the abbey's intellectual life and provided the basis for its vitality in the thirteenth century. Books were produced on a scale such as to suggest that St Albans intended to assume the role of a

newer glossed texts from Paris

contacts with the Continental schools

(opposite)
The first five verses of St Luke's Gospel, with gloss. The script is an early Gothic text hand, written at St Albans Abbey at the end of the twelfth century. Cambridge, Trinity College Library MS B.5.3, folio 111 verso

50

B. Lucas: de omnibz que
fecit ihc & docuit usq; in diem
qua assumptꝰ est sermone fa
cturus: pmo eoꝝ qui de eo fal
sa scripsert redarguit aud̴
eram. Scribit au
tem: hystorico
stilo. Magis enī
in describendis
rebz. qm in exprī
mendis precep
tis studium ha
bunt. & hystori
co more. de nar
ratione sumpsit
plena digestione
psequitur.

tas predicandi falsa. qui sub
nomine aptorum: conati sē
sectas perfi
die inducere.

B. Mul
ti conati
sunt. Ho
ta ea ma
xime cau
sa scrip
sisse euā
gelium:
ne pseu
do euan
gelistis os
set facul
falsa scripserunt.

Ut basilides
mul
rappelles: 7
qui sub no
a co
mine tho
nati
me. ul' ma
sunt
thie: uel a
ordi
liorum apo
nare
stolorum:
nar
rationem que
Non nos: sed in nobis: dc̄s fecit.

B. Multa ñ
tam numerosi
tate: qm heresy
diuersitate.

Iacobꝝ. o
natur: qui inci
pit nec pficit.
qui suis uirrbz
non grē dei q̄r
rigat confidit.
qui qd ab ali
is dictum ui
det: abolere
intendit. Hon
conat̄: q̄ diuino
spū res ī dicta
mīnstīnt̄c cep
ta complet.

Quod re
dundat: nul
li deficit. &
te completo:
nullus dubi
tat. cum fi
dem: effectus
astruit. erit̄
probat.

didicerunt que scribe
rent. s; etiam iohs īma
theus multa de infan
tia. pueria. genealogia
saluatoris: alis narran
tibus didicerunt

in nobis cōple
dun dant. Euangely.
te sunt rerum:

B. Tra
diderut.
Hon solū
marcus
& lucas
auditu

sicut aq
didert
nobis qui ab ini
ao ipsi
Hon solum corpo
uiderut.
ut portui
raliter. sed etiam men
& mini
ns intuitu

Iacobꝝ. cō
plete st. Redun
dant. puniuer
sum mundū:
mites fidelium
rigant & confir
mant.

Iacobꝝ. 1
derunt. Genu
naturē est in
homine pfe
cto. intentio
& actio. unā q̄

publishing house for the distribution in England of Continental scholarship.

Scribe B, for example, working under Abbot Simon, made efforts to standardize the abbey's library books by providing tables of contents and running titles in the books produced. This can be placed in the context of the ample evidence for organizing knowledge on the Continent. We can see the furthering of the impulse to compile library catalogues, of varying degrees of sophistication, which had received its first impetus in the Carolingian period. In Paris, for example, is preserved the catalogue of the library of the north French abbey of St Amand, compiled in about 1160 by Walter, librarian of that abbey. Walter annotated his catalogue with notes concerning the provenance of the 221 books in the abbey's library when he took office, and added the list of 110 volumes he himself had been responsible for adding to the abbey's holdings. A catalogue such as this provides a useful comparison with the achievement of the abbey of St Albans.

The international contacts of the house are further indicated by the lavish decoration, for it was executed in this period by a single team of itinerant artists, possibly secular craftsmen who settled at the abbey for one or two decades and some of whom worked also for other centres during that period, such as Mont St Michel in Normandy, and Winchester. At least four masters and their assistants executed

organizing knowledge

lavish decoration

(opposite)
The Epistles of St Paul, glossed by Peter Lombard, copied at St Albans Abbey in the last quarter of the twelfth century, probably under Abbot Simon. This page has the thirteenth-century *ex libris* note in the top margin: Hic est liber Sancti Albani (This book belongs to St Albans Abbey). Cambridge, Trinity College Library MS O.5.8, folio 2 recto.

PAVLVS
SERV

IHV XPI uo
catus apts
segatus
in euange
lium dei.

appellatioe ap gcos . i . quiete . ...
appellatiuū . ap gcos . hebreos . ...
aplicos . anno passiōis . ɂ resurrē ...
passiōe aplatum gentiu cū ...
lus a saule psecutore . qr sic ill ...
iuxta ɂdictū aploɀ ad magist ...
seruit augtinus sic dices . ɧ ō ...
ostendet paruū tanqm minu ...
tia aliqua nom ſ mutauit ap ...
lum . ɱ . modic ÷ . Immutatū ...
. i . quietū . qui eni pri tēptatiōe ...
id fecisse phibetur . qui mitru ...
nom . ut cephas . ɂ filij tontrui ...
quos incathedra beati pet sub ...
sce ecclie contulit . ſ . a paulo se ...
sic partic qui parchos su paui ...
pus subiuigauit . paulus sit app ...
ditur . mag placet qɂ inɂa ɂſue ...
binit . alios trns usos ee nōib ÷ ...
uocat ÷ ɂ mathe qui ɂ leui dici ...
nob ɂ paulus duplici uoctat ...
ū euidenr ostēdit sɂptura ū ...
assignat . ɧ ieronimo aū ...
incɂptari di . quē ɂ dñs ip . uas eletiōis uocauit . ɂ ta ...
s ; qrendū ÷ cur seruus dicat . qui alibi sēpsit . ɧon ...
s . lib . ɂ dñs aplis att . Iam ñ dicam uos seruos . ſ . ami ...
ɂ pene seruit . ɂ ÷ seruiɂ amoɂis . ɂ filiatioⁿis . atqɂ hui ...
si gɂ sed id humilitatis ɂ amouis seruitute dictū p ...
ōi libtate nobilioɂ ÷ seruiɂ X . dicendo ɡ seruus n ...
ɂ ne misera seruiɂ uideat . ñ simpliciɂ att . seruɂ . ſ . addi ...
÷ regnare . ɧic ū hebraice . socher gɂe latine . saluatoɂ ...
pptm suū a peccis eoɀ add . xɂi . i . regis ɂ sacdotis . xɂo ...
reges ɂ sacdotes ungebant . Xpc aū unct ÷ ñ oleo uiſ ...
deus . d . τ . o . l . h nom alijs olim fuɂt adiectm . ſ . iɧu fc ...
a lege fcōɂ se exiuit ostend . ɂ utriqɂ nom ponendo . i . u ...
ɡ iɧm altm ū xpm suspicarem fuisse . ſ . unū ɂ eũ ...
ecce de humili fcs ÷ altius . at si ilt supɂ quibɂ sebeb ...
iuos humiles sitis . ut exaltemiⁿ . qui . ɱ . se humili ...
uocat . qɂ ñ a se ueniens tanɡ ɂmet honoɂe sume ...

itinerant artists

export to other centres

(opposite)
The canon tables from
a Glossed Gospel Book
written at St Albans
Abbey at the end of the
twelfth century.
Cambridge, Trinity
College Library MS
B.5.3, folio 2 recto

the illumination of St Albans' grandest books, including the 'Alexis Master', the 'Apocrypha Master', and possibly the 'Lambeth Bible Master', so called after the most famous books in which their work can be seen. A group of itinerant artists working in a particular atelier is a phenomenon one occasionally encounters in the early middle ages. Another example is the group of artists responsible for the so-called 'palace-school' manuscripts of the Frankish king Charles the Bald in the 860s and 870s. We thus have the monks and patrons wanting the best craftsmen available for their books and bringing in masters from outside to do the work they wanted, just as, in this century, the monks of Ampleforth commissioned David Kindersley's Workshop to inscribe the foundation stone for their new building and the clergy of St Albans called on the workshop for the chapter house slate.

Remarkable illustrations and historiated initials were added to the books, of which the glossed Gospel texts with their sumptuously ornamented paintings in a manuscript now in Cambridge are a representative example. Fine illuminated manuscripts, moreover, were clearly produced for export to other centres and individuals elsewhere in England as well as for local use, such as the Hildesheim Psalter copied for Christina of Markyate, a book remarkable for a range of

54

Canon nonus

Lucas	Johannes
xxx	cc xiv
xxv	cc xxii
cc lxii	c xii
cc lxii	c xviii
cc lxxiii	cc xxvii
cc lxxiii	cc xxix
cc lxxiii	cc xxxi
ccc iii	c xc
ccc vii	c xc
ccc xii	c xc
ccc iii	c lxxvi
ccc vii	c lxxvi
ccc xii	c lxxvi
ccc iii	c lxxii
ccc vii	c lxxii
ccc xii	c lxxii
ccc xl	cc xiii
ccc xl	cc xvii
ccc vli	cc xxi
ccc xli	cc xxiii
ccc xli	cc xxv

Canon x.

Math	Math
ii	ccc xxvii
iiii	ccc xlv
vi	ccc li
xii	ccc lv
xxiiii	T lvii.
xxvi	
xxix	
xxxiii	

Ca. xi. Marc.

Math	Marc.
xxxv	xix
xxxvii	xxxi
xxx ix	xliii
xlii	xlvi
xlv	lviii
lii	lxii
lvi	lxx
lxxv	lxxiii
lxxxi	lxxvi
lxxxix	lxxxviii
xci	xc
xcix	xcii
ci	xciiii
c vi	ci
c ix	c iiii
c xii	c xxiii
c xv	

iconography with striking debts to the book painting of the previous two centuries. Quite apart from their contents therefore, these books are works of art and monuments to great skill in their own right. A large proportion of the books produced for export to other places were works relating to the monastic liturgy and there appears to have been a massive programme undertaken to replace all the service books of the abbey in the later twelfth century. This coincided with the erection and completion of the new church building and its dedication in 1166.

From the Chronica Maiora of Matthew Paris, written and illustrated at St Albans Abbey in the thirteenth century. This is the elephant sent by King Louis IX of France to King Henry III in 1255, and its keeper. Cambridge, Corpus Christi College Library MS 16, folio 152 verso

If St Albans was preeminent for its book production in the twelfth and early thirteenth centuries, it was for the writing of national and international history that it became famous in the later thirteenth and the fourteenth centuries, with the works of Roger of Wendover, Matthew Paris, John of Wallingford, William Rishanger and Thomas of Walsingham. This flowering of literary activity was, as Rodney Thomson has noted, relatively late in comparison with other English houses. But it is to Matthew Paris that we owe most of our detailed information about St Albans and its abbots once they had taken office. His famous Chronicle was complemented by the engaging *Gesta Abbatum* which was devoted to an account of his own community and, if prejudiced and gossipy, is also notable for its sustained emphasis on books and learning. Written in the 1240s and 1250s, it was extended in the fifteenth century by Thomas of Walsingham, and Matthew Paris's autograph manuscript of the work survives in London. In compiling his account, Matthew Paris declares his indebtedness to 'the ancient roll of Bartholomew the clerk who for a long time had been servant to Adam the Cellarer'. Adam the Cellarer, one of the very few members of the community who was not an abbot but who was nevertheless honoured with burial in the chapter house, died not long after 1161. The fact that he

the writing of history

Matthew Paris

was buried with the abbots rather than with the other monks, suggests the regard in which he was held as historian of his community before 1166. It is to him that the account for the years 1140-1166, preserved by Matthew Paris, is to be credited. Adam clearly kept a record of those matters which most concerned him in his position, such as the material acquisitions and losses occasioned by the day to day running of the community and its domestic household affairs, details of each abbot's acquisition of land and privileges, gifts made to the church of plate, vestments and precious books, and the appropriation of funds for the materials needed in the scriptorium and payment of the visiting master artists, as well as his personal observations about the spiritual and intellectual stature of the abbots he served.

gifts made to the church

The literary activity of the twelfth, thirteenth and fourteenth centuries, moreover, as well as the established contacts with European intellectual developments, continued into the fifteenth century, and under Abbot John Whethamstede [1452-65] the abbey became a centre for the new humanism. Only with the dissolution of the monasteries under Henry VIII was St Albans eclipsed and the work of its abbots forgotten for a time. May this new memorial to them revive the memory of their greatness, of their cultural achievements, and of the patronage they

(opposite)
The commentary on Leviticus by Hesychius of Jerusalem. Hesychius wrote in Greek in the fifth century but his commentary was translated into Latin in the sixth century. This copy of the Latin version was made at Christ Church Canterbury in the twelfth century. Cambridge, Trinity College Library MS B.2.9, folio 14 recto

offered both then and now for the craftsmen commissioned to commemorate them: reminders of both their intellectual and artistic interests, and their devotion to the Christian faith.

devotion to the Christian faith

& uitulox: s; p ppnu sanguine. ingref
suf e. semel in sca, eterna redempno
ne inuenta. Ec rursus. Neq; eni in
manu factam ingreffus est xpc forma
uftrox: S; in ipm celu. ad ostendendu
se uiltui di pro nob; hic g tabnaclin
testimonii celu. quippe quia in ipo ha
bitare din xphe testificati sunt. intelli
gam. Qui habitat in do in celis. irride
bit eos. & nemo ascendit in celu nisi
qui descendit de celo. unigenit' de se
metipo dicit hominib;. Ibi sanguine
introduxit. quia cicatrices portans
passionu. a mortuis resurrexit. Vnde
& suu corp palpandu thome pbuit.
atq; ita in celum ascendit. pbant aute
seqntia. Cuiq; intinxerit digitu san
guine. aspget de eo septief cora dno
cotra uelum sciarii. multis nominib;
carne dni appellat. qa & multas opa
tiones impleuit. Vnde & ipe dris. in
quide semetipm sacrificiu. in pastoe.
Deinde rursus uita. & pane uite. & g
nu tritici. Opportune dispensatonis ab
uarians. suas appellationes nomina
uit. Ct nuc g uelum. ei carne appellaui.

Ous multis notib; caro xpi
appellee i qd intris ex in
firmitate mouens offerebat
se ipm sibi i celo
ex uittate.

59

Inscription for the entrance of the Benedictine abbey at Ampleforth

SEEK FIRST THE KINGDOM OF GOD

PATRICK BARRY O.S.B.

HOC IPSO IN LOCO

DOMVM ILLAM QVAM ANNA FAIRFAX

FEMINA ILLVSTRIS CASTELLI GILLING DOMINA

CAPELLANO SVO D ANSELMO BOLTON EXSTRVXERAT

FRATRES RELIQI LAVRENTIANI ex DEI CVSTODIA PVLSI

DECENNIO POST SIBI CONCESSAM INCOLVERE

ATQVE IBIDEM VITAM CONVENTVALEM

REDINTEGRAVERVNT

ANNO SALVTIS NOSTRAE

MDCCCII

TRADITION

The Benedictine abbeys of the middle ages were so unlike any institution of which we have experience today that it is very easy to miss the point and judge them wrongly. Only by first carefully separating the different strands in their make-up can we come to a realistic understanding. St Albans Abbey was one of the greatest and most influential of the many English abbeys. Little remains of it except the church. That church is now called a cathedral, but it was not built as such. To begin our understanding we must forget the notion of 'cathedral'. We must see it rather as the centre of a Benedictine abbey. It was the focus, the raison d'être of a large community of monks who were dedicated to the worship of God and to prayer in that church. They celebrated there with solemnity and sacred music the Mass and seven times in the day and once in the night the 'office' of psalms and readings from Scripture which was the framework of their worship. The local people, visitors and guests shared in this worship. It was for this monastic round of prayer that the church was built and maintained. We must see the size, the proportions and the rich decorations, which are now all gone, as an expression of the profound importance attached to that worship which the monks, following St Benedict, called 'the work of God'.

carefully separating the different strands

forget the notion of 'cathedral'

monastic round of prayer

'the work of God'

63

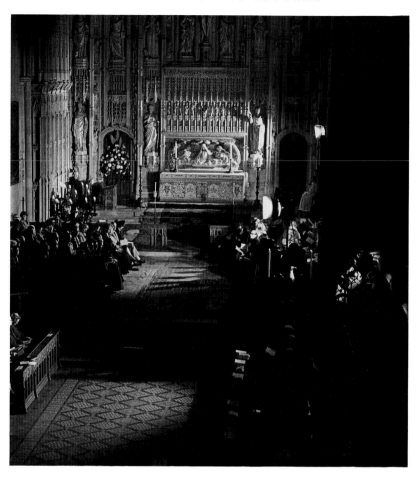

The dedication of the slate in St Albans Abbey

Then we must understand that the laymen, who were founders and benefactors and who endowed the abbey and enriched it, did so because of the spiritual value they put on that prayer, that 'work of God' to which the monks were committed. To them it was so important that they thought *blessing to* of their gift as being of benefit and a *everyone* blessing to everyone. The local people, the

64

guests, the poor and the pilgrims who came to the abbey did not disagree. They all had a share in 'the work of God'. They were inspired, helped in trouble and in need, spiritually sustained by the prayer and life of the Abbey. Next to worship itself that help and inspiration was what the abbey was for. All who wanted could share in it.

help and inspiration

In this way an abbey became an integral part of the social fabric - an integral part because society in those days was a believing Christian society. As this happened another strand in the make-up of a mediaeval abbey appeared. It was the strand of power, influence and status. In feudal society a great abbey acquired a stake of its own in the country's system of administration, with its many interlocking rights and obligations, which held society together. The Normans especially required their abbeys to fulfil this role. It was in connection with this role and all it implied that the influence of society on the Benedictine abbeys was often a serious threat to their original spiritual idea and purpose. Hence inevitably there were times when the work of God was obscured and distorted by the scheming of men.

it was the strand of power, influence and status

distorted by the scheming of men

But there was more to a great mediaeval abbey than prayer and politics. Yet other strands of great benefit and lasting value developed from the ordered rhythm of the daily life of the monks. Their life involved study and so they cherished books in their

The Latin version of the Commentary on Leviticus by Hesychius of Jerusalem, copied at Canterbury in the twelfth century. Cambridge, Trinity College Library MS B.2.9, folio 56 verso

libraries. They copied books also for their own use and to meet the demands of others. They had schools in their monasteries to teach young monks, and in these schools lay children were often taught to read and write. There were scholars among the monks; and there were writers also among them of all sorts from Anselm of Bec and Canterbury with his high learning and original thought to Matthew Paris of St Albans who was both a competent chronicler and a mediaeval gossip columnist. There were great builders and craftsmen also among the monks. They were farmers also who cared for the land and managed it well. Not all the creative work, however, whether of building, decoration, painting or craftsmanship was done by the monks

they copied books

high learning and original thought

Inscription carved by
Dom Patrick Barry

O R A T E
PRO ANIMIS NOSTRORUM
IN BELLO DEFUNCTORUM
MCMXXXIX · MCMXLIV

67

themselves. Laymen - the contemporary masters of illumination, carving in wood and stone, coloured glass-making, building, the binding of books, the making of furniture, weaving, dyeing - might at any time find employment at the great abbeys. In this way monks became patrons of art and the employers of craftsmen. Their great churches also were welcoming and colourful and became centres where ordinary people became familiar with the work of great artists and craftsmen.

patrons of art and the employers of craftsmen

At another level there was a strand in the monks' daily life which was of great importance. This was the care and support they gave to the poor, the destitute, the homeless. This care was integral to an abbey's life, with an important official charged to sustain it. Every abbey had also an Infirmary for sick monks and it often became a medical centre also for the neighbourhood, where herbal remedies and experience and expertise in dealing with acute problems were available.

care and support they gave to the poor

All these main strands of the monks' daily life and many others of less significance were woven round the most important strand of all - the central core. This was the rule of life given by St Benedict which he modestly called a 'basic rule for beginners' but which has proved of lasting value, so that even today it is used and revived in modern publications as a helpful guide not only for monks but also for laymen and women seeking to live a

the rule of life given by St Benedict

true Christian life. We should not be surprised at that because St Benedict's Rule is a mirror of New Testament teaching.

Inscription on the monks' vault in Monks' Wood, Ampleforth, carved by Dom Patrick Barry

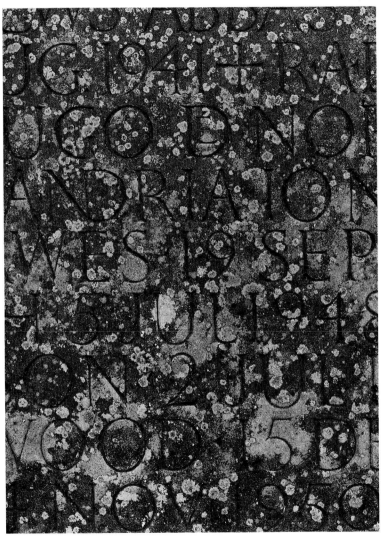

> ·II· QVALIS DEBEAT ESSE ABBAS ·
>
> Abbas qui prae esse dignus e. monasterio. semper meminisse debet quod dicitur et nomen maioris factis Implere. Xpi enim agere uices Inmonasterio creditur. quando Ipsius uocatur prae noie. Dicente apto. Accepistis spm adoptionis filionum. Inquo clamamus abba pat. Ideoq. abbas nihil extra praecepti dni q absit. debet aut docere. aut constituere uel iubere. Sed iussio eius uel doctrina. fermentum diuine Iustitie. In discipulorum mentib; conspargat. Meminit Semper

A copy of the Rule of St Benedict written at St Augustine's Canterbury in the mid-tenth century showing the chapter on the qualities of the abbot. Cambridge, Trinity College Library O.2.30, folio 134 recto

its greatest challenge is to the Abbot

The Rule's fundamental theme is the true and sincere seeking of God. It is to teach monks how to serve God. It is moderate and balanced in what it demands. Its greatest challenge is to the Abbot. It urges him to rule in such a way that he will be loved rather than feared. It counsels him to think of how different individuals are in the guidance they need, to care especially for those in trouble, to put spiritual considerations always before material. It says that monks should put nothing before the love of Christ, and see Christ especially in those who most need help and care like the elderly and the young. It lays down

70

that hospitality is an essential work of a monastery and tells the Abbot that guests must be received as though they were Christ himself. It divides the monks' day between prayer, reflective reading or study and manual work, through which it expects them to earn their living. It speaks of the respect with which monks must treat not only people but things also - the very tools and common property of the monastery. It insists that the most important work of all, to which everything must give way, is the work of God - their common worship in the abbey church and prayer for all Christian peoples. At the end St Benedict speaks of the spirit which should inspire all that goes on in a monastery. It is not to be a spirit of bitterness which leads to harm and evil, but a strong, affirming, life-giving spirit; a spirit of mutual forbearance and understanding, of sympathy for weakness, of purity, of charity, of seeking to satisfy not personal ambition but the needs of others. This is the spirit, he says, which will bring us all to eternal life.

hospitality is an essential work of a monastery

affirming, life-giving spirit

In this central strand of the Rule is the heart and inspiration of the life of a Benedictine abbey. In the long history of monasticism there have been times when it has been masked or distorted. Other strands, other influences have obscured it. In the end either the ideals it expressed reassert themselves and there is new life in that community or it comes to an end. It

71

remains the one essential inspiration of a monastic house. Wherever it is found in widely differing circumstances, in large monasteries or small, in monasteries of men or of women, among their oblates also in lay life, there the true Benedictine spirit survives and helps men and women to spiritual fulfilment and peace in Christ.

the true Benedictine spirit survives

The true history, then, of a great abbey like St Albans is largely hidden. It is concerned with the fidelity or infidelity at any time of the community and of the individuals who formed it to the great spiritual ideal which they professed. Their history, therefore, is not unlike the history of the chosen people and of the Church which Christ founded. It had its high moments and its low; but so long as it preserved the ideal and sought to return to it, there was hope. And where there is hope, there is life and development.

preserved the ideal

72

INSCRIPTION

And also of
ROBERT OF THE CHAMBER
father of Pope Adrian IV
ADAM THE CELLARER
Prior ADAM WITTENHAM
ADAM ROUS
Surgeon to Edward III

Prior ADAM

ADA

Surgeon

VIEZERD

REMOVE

INSCRIPTION

When my mother and father first married they lived in St Albans. I mention this fact because I have always felt there is some subterranean connection between myself and the place and particularly the abbey. Of course this may have been built up in my mind by my parents – not on purpose but simply because they loved St Albans and the abbey. Moreover there used to be a large painting of a pageant which depicted

some connection between myself & the abbey

The painting by Frank O. Salisbury showing the passing of Queen Eleanor, with David Kindersley's father seated on the horse on the left

my father as St George riding on a white horse through the streets of St Albans. This meant frequent visits as a child to show relations and friends the picture. This painting always filled me with pride and when I learnt that it had been stolen I was appalled. It was not, however, a very good piece of work. One wonders why anybody should want it – apart from me.

frequent visits as a child

My other reason for feeling so close to St Albans was the Roman mosaics which were being unearthed in the meadows beneath the abbey. This closeness arose because from the age of one I was living at Welwyn and under our garden was a Roman cemetery. From about the age of four I was allowed by my father to remove

the Roman mosaics

David Kindersley drawing out a slate with a washable pencil

76

earth from the burial urns until stronger hands could lift them clear. I so much wanted to find a Roman mosaic, like the ones at St Albans. I did, however, come across a Samian plate which had the maker's name stamped on the underneath. This lettering VIRTVS FECIT may well have provided the soil of my profession.

the soil of my profession

So, when my sister brought the news that the Dean of St Albans wanted me to design and cut an inscription for the abbots that had been unearthed, I was more than ready to undertake the work. Their removal to the centre of the abbey had been agreed and a stone with their names was required. As soon as I received the list of names my interest increased. Several had

I was more than ready

The first draft for the inscription

names associated with villages in
Hertfordshire and adjacent counties and
some related to places across the Channel.
There was nothing anonymous about
them. Their names were truly worthy of a
fine memorial and I hoped my design

their noble lives   would be able to live up to their noble lives.

Peter Moore, the Dean, whom I had
known at Ely, was just as enthusiastic as I,
if not more so. Andrew Anderson the
architect guided me through the design and

the site was not   so the project grew in quality. The site was
easy   not altogether an easy one. For example the

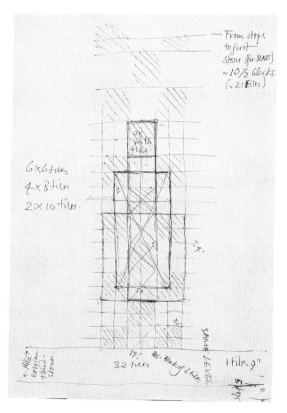

*Trying out different
sizes of slate to fit with
the tile pattern*

burials needed a grave some 10'6" long
and the floor which was to take the
memorial was three steps higher than
where people would stand in order to read
the inscription. Consequently it was
necessary to increase the height of the
letters the farther they were from the
reader. I also wanted to thicken the serifs *thicken the serifs*
for the same reason, but this was decided
against. The fear was that the inscription
would not be sufficiently Trajan. To show
the effect of increasing the height of the
letters to counter the perspective I *counter the*
suggested holding the drawing in a *perspective*
horizontal position close to the eye, thus
the letters would be seen to appear the
same height and easily legible over the
whole length of the inscription.

    I sent off the drawing with the following
explanatory letter.

Dear Peter, *David Kindersley's*
It is not often that everything fits together *letter to Peter Moore*
to form one whole, and this idea I had for *the Dean of St Albans*
the abbots may have to go because of my *explaining the design*
inability to express in words the idea *17 September 1979*
behind the design. Should this be the case,
I will try a design 36" wide by 90", but it
will be dull by comparison.

    To clear away the simple things first.
The floor is tiled; four tiles make a complete
pattern and the centre of the pattern is
bisected by the centre of the abbey.
Therefore the size of the hole to receive the
slate is limited – it must be 2 tiles or 6 tiles

HERE

REST THE MORTAL

REMAINS OF

GEOFFREY OF GORHAM

PAUL OF CAEN

RICHARD D'ALBINI

RALPH OF GUBION

ROBERT OF GORRON

SIMON

WARIN OF CAMBRIDGE

JOHN DE CELLA

WILLIAM OF TRUMPINGTON

JOHN OF HERTFORD

JOHN DE LA MOOTE

and also of

ROBERT OF THE CAMERA

Father of Pope Adrian IV

ADAM THE CELLARER

ADAM WITTENHAM

PRIOR ADAM ROUS

Surgeon to Edward III

Removed from

THE CHAPTER HOUSE

The first plan for the layout, quickly sketched

HERE
REST THE MORTAL
REMAINS OF ABBOTS ← 1077 – 1401
PAUL OF CAEN 1
RICHARD D'ALBINI 2
GEOFFREY OF GORRON 3
RALPH OF GUBION 4
ROBERT OF GORRON 5
SIMON 6
WARIN OF CAMBRIDGE 7
JOHN DE CELLA 8
WILLIAM 9
OF TRUMPINGTON 10
JOHN OF HERTFORD 10
JOHN DE LA MOOTE 11 ← 1401
AND ALSO OF 12
ROBERT OF THE CAMERA 13
Father of Pope Adrian IV
ADAM THE CELLARER
ADAM WITTENHAM
PRIOR ADAM ROUS
Surgeon to Edward III
REMOVED FROM
THE CHAPTER HOUSE
1978.
SEEK YE FIRST
THE KINGDOM OF
GOD

Dates

The next step was to
try to fit the layout for
the inscription into the
preferred tall format of
the slate

wide, that is, 18": or 54". It might be argued that a half pattern could remain round the slate, in which case we are talking about 4 tiles wide, that is, 36". In the former case one must not, I am sure, *the length of the Abbey* violate aesthetically the length of the Abbey or that particular site with an horizontal or square design. And it is unlikely that a slate 54" wide could be found to make 72" long, let alone 90". In the latter case, we might obtain a 36" wide slate 90" long – but not 108". We would still be stuck with a vertical list and all the letters would be *the gut feeling* smaller. Now to come to the gut feeling. I am sorry about the drawing, but the lettering is classical Roman except for the E in REST (this can be changed) but I like it. The inscription has been conceived in the best classical traditions. The Trajan *in the best classical traditions* inscription allows for the fact that the letters at the top are further from the viewer. Top letters are $4^1/2$" and those in the last line $3^7/8$". The letters in my inscription on the west wall of Trinity Ante-Chapel lose $5/8$" as the eye travels from top to bottom. Both these inscriptions have letters that are visually the same size, and in the case of the Trinity War Memorial the letters get narrower in relation to their height progressively towards the top.

In the 108" x 18" inscription proposed for St Albans the requirements are much more extreme. The vast numbers of people visiting the abbey need something really rather striking and unusual to attract their attention – length and narrowness help to do this. Moreover, ceremonially speaking, it has a function in that processions will tend to divide themselves quite naturally either side of the slate. But the people, the tourist, the wanderer, will always or nearly always be viewing the slate at an angle far in excess of the classical inscription mentioned. Consequently I have made an increase in the letter size from 2" to $3^1/4$" at the top. If one lays the drawing flat on a table and really has one's eye about 4" above the point indicated, and then looks at the closest R first of all, which is in every way classical, one will see that the R's above all have the same form. When this inscription is viewed from within the chancel, the letters at the beginning will have, it is true, the characteristics of Rustic Roman letters. It must be remembered that Rustic Roman letters were used just as much as the Classical. As a compromise, I would keep all serifs as on the full size. However, the difference between the letters on my drawing and those of Roman times is that the Trajan Inscription was cut circa 104 AD and we now live 1875 years later – whatever that may mean!

Of course, I don't know what feelings people have about the abbots. For me though, their bones represent a long period of time when life was much harder than today, and yet truth and understanding evolution walked hand in hand. How else

length and narrowness

Rustic Roman letters

truth and understanding evolution

83

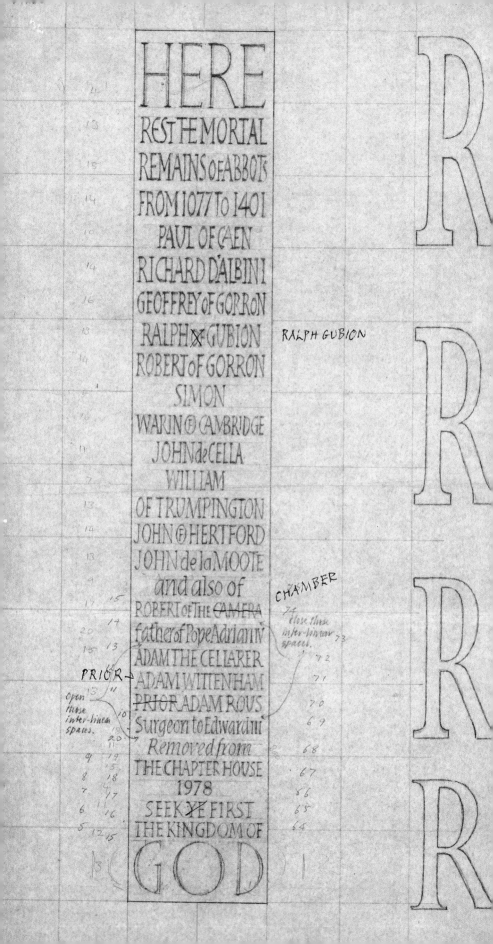

HERE
REST THE MORTAL
REMAINS OF ABBOTS
FROM 1077 TO 1401
PAUL OF CAEN
RICHARD D'ALBINI
GEOFFREY OF GORRON
RALPH ✗ GUBION
ROBERT OF GORRON
SIMON
WARIN ⊙ CAMBRIDGE
JOHN de CELLA
WILLIAM
OF TRUMPINGTON
JOHN ⊙ HERTFORD
JOHN de la MOOTE
and also of
ROBERT OF THE ~~CAMERA~~
father of Pope Adrian IV
ADAM THE CELLARER
ADAM WITTENHAM
~~PRIOR~~ ADAM ROUS
Surgeon to Edward III
Removed from
THE CHAPTER HOUSE
1978
SEEK YE FIRST
THE KINGDOM OF
GOD

RALPH GUBION

CHAMBER
74
close these
inter-linear
spaces.
73
72
71
70
69
68
67
66
65
64

PRIOR →
Open
these
inter-linear
spaces.

can one explain the faith that evolved new architecture, new forms of art and the word. I shall never forget having Warin of Cambridge's fine skull in my hands, and the interesting example of physical de-volution in the over-bite of today.
Yours ever, David.

Warin of Cambridge's fine skull

As the Dean was away the letter was answered by the architect.

Dear David,
I am writing in the Dean's absence to ask you to put the slate inscription in hand. The Cardinal's visit is on 21st November.

Reply from the Architect
14 September 1979

I know from your letter of 17th September that you are giving the amendments Peter has suggested careful thought. The increase in size the Architect's Liaison Committee feel is desirable is, I think, important to emphasise the fact that the remains of not just two or three but over a dozen abbots lie beneath the stone: it is quite a number! As a lover of good lettering, I very much want this to be one of the sights of the Abbey.

lover of good lettering

The idea of using letters of decreasing size is a very good one and I am glad that all the serifs are to be the same. At its meeting last Thursday, the Cathedral Council asked that the YE be omitted in the third line from the end and there was also, I understand, comment on the conjoined THE in the full-size drawing: this would also apply to the second line from the top.

letters of decreasing size

(opposite)
This was the final sketch which was approved and from which David worked, although the slate was twice as wide as indicated in this sketch

Perhaps the extra width gained by going to four tiles wide will make some easing of this possible. I also wonder if the ordinary tourist not used to classical Roman inscriptions will find the abbreviations of OF difficult to take in at first glance.

creative suggestions

I hope you will find these suggestions creative. For your encouragement, may I say that nothing produced by a craftsman of your distinction could ever be dull.
Yours sincerely, Andrew Anderson

difficulties were resolved

All these difficulties were resolved one way or the other. On the whole I believe that the persons commissioning one's work should dictate more than generally believed, because their input to the job allows for expression linked to the period we are in. Anyway I am not so obsessional as to feel otherwise.

welsh slate

The 10'6" welsh slate agreed upon was ordered from Mr Lloyd of Wincilate Limited. Because of modern quarrying techniques we could not get the length in one piece; it had to be in two. Because of this it was much easier to man-handle. The drawing out on the slate could now begin

what fun we had

and what fun we had. As far as possible I wanted the letters to be predominately equal, but because one was dealing with names, and some were short, I centralised them. The width of the slate was 36" with a large margin on each side to offset the decorative floor tiles all around the slate.

the drawing on the slate

The drawing on the slate took some weeks

This picture shows the sketchy way in which we set out the inscription. Usually it does not look so neat. At this stage questions of layout and spelling are taken care of

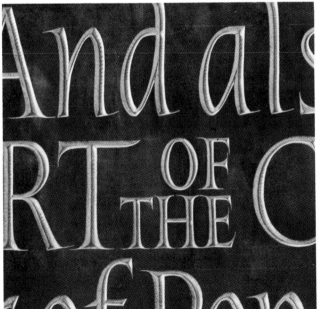

Here you can see how the final decisions of shaping and spacing the letter forms have been made during the actual cutting of the letter. This way the creation of the inscription is the living moment at which you hit the chisel – here, literally, is the 'incisive moment'.

of trying different ligatures. Ligatures, the joining of letters, are interesting. Some join quite naturally and others are impossible.

Every name had to fit the width of the slate, and be centred

lettering with ligatures

we also used 'nesting' letters

To have your lettering with ligatures requires everything to be drawn out before cutting starts. They must somehow be in tune. Apart from ligatures we also used 'nesting' letters. These need not join but fit into each other, as in Warin of Cambridge.

Lida and I had weeks of trying out different combinations and organizing which was best. Sometimes we agreed a combination in principle and Lida cut it her own way. Anybody dropping into the workshop was asked for their opinion and changes were made right up to the final blow of hammer onto chisel.

For five months the workshop was in the hold of the abbots of St Albans; we hope that we were aiming then, as we do still, for the same perfection to which they devoted their entire lives.

Lida cutting an inscription

HERE
REST THE MORTAL
REMAINS ⊕ ABBOTS
· FROM 1077 To 1401
· PAUL OF CAEN ·
RICHARD d'ALBINI
GEoFFREY⊕GoRRoN
· RALPH GUBION ·
ROBERT of GORRON
· SIMON ·
WARIN ⊕ CAMBRIDGE
· JOHN de CELLA ·
WILLIAM
OF TRUMPINGToN
JOHN ⊕ HERTFORD
JOHN de la MOOTE
And also of
RoBERT of the CHAMBeR
father of Pope Adrian IV
ADAM THE CELLARER
Prior ADaM WiTTeNHAM
ADAM ROUS
Surgeon to Edward III

REMOVED in 1978 from
The CHAPTER HOUSE

SEEK FIRST
THE KINGDOM OF
GOD

The slate as cut
showing how every
letter increased by
1mm in each line,
gaining over an inch in
height overall, but
remaining the same
width. The cross bars
of H, E, A etc. were
thickened in
proportion

(opposite)
The stone *in situ*,
photographed as seen,
which shows how the
perspective is adjusted
to ensure the entire
inscription is legible

HERE

REST THE MORTAL
REMAINS ℗ ABBOTs
FROM 1077 To 1401
· PAUL OF CAEN ·
RICHARD d'ALBINI
GEoFFReY ℗ GoRRoN
· RALPH GUBION ·
ROBERT of GORRON
· SIMON ·
WARIN ℗ CAMBRIDGE
JOHN de CELLA
WILLIAM
OF TRUMPINGToN
JOHN ℗ HERTFORD
JOHN de la MOOTE

And also of
RoBERT of the CHAMBeR
father of Pope Adrian IV
ADAM the CELLARER
Prior ADaM WitteNHAM
ADAM ROUS
Surgeon to Edward III

REMOVED in 1978 from
The CHAPTER HOUSE

SEEK FIRST
THE KINGDOM OF
GOD

ACKNOWLEDGEMENTS

For permission to reproduce illustrations from manuscripts in their possession we are grateful to the following:
The Bodleian Library, Oxford (Laud misc. 409, folio 3 verso)
The University Library, Durham (Bishop Cosin's Library, MS V.III.1, fol. 22 verso)
The Master and Fellows of Corpus Christi College, Cambridge (MS 16, fol. 152 verso)
The Master and Fellows of Trinity College, Cambridge (B.2.9. folios 14 recto and 56 verso; B.5.1, folio 47 verso; B.5.3, folios 2 recto, 46 recto and 111 verso, O.2.30, folios 130 recto and 134 recto; O.5.8, folio 2 recto)
Trinity College, Dublin (MS 177, folio 60 recto)
The British Library, London (Cotton Claudius D.vi, folio 12 verso)

For the illustrations of the dedication ceremony, of the Salisbury painting and of the slate itself, we wish to thank the Verulamium Museum, St Albans
For the illustrations of the Ampleforth inscriptions we thank Julia Hedgecoe
For the illustrations of the excavation and the plans of the burials we are grateful to Professors Martin Biddle and Birthe Kjølbye-Biddle
For the photographs of David and Lida we thank Michael Manni
For proofreading we should like to thank Professor E J Kenney, David McKitterick and Peter Moore, the Dean of St Albans

CHRONOLOGICAL TABLE

The history of St Albans	Reigning monarch
Foundation of St Albans Abbey	Offa of Mercia, 757-796
Monastic reform at St Albans and acceptance of the Rule of St Benedict under Abbot Aelfric *circa* 970	Edgar, king of Mercia from 957 and king of England, 959-975
1066 Conquest of England by the Normans	Harald II Godwinesson, 1066 William I, the Conqueror, 1066-1087
1077 First Norman abbot appointed, Paul of Caen, 1077-97. Dependent cells established at Wallingford, Tynemouth, Belvoir, Hertford and Binham. First chapter house built	William II Rufus, 1087-1100
Foundation of the abbey scriptorium Second Norman abbot, Richard d'Albini, 1097-1119	Henry I, 1100-1135
Dependent cells established at Wymondham, Hatfield and Millbrook	
Geoffrey of Gorron, abbot 1119-1146 The 'great leap forward' in book production Ralph Gobion, abbot 1146-1151	Stephen, 1135-1154
Robert of Gorron, abbot 1151-1167 The building of the second chapter house Simon, abbot 1167-1183 1180 death of Adam the Cellarer Warin of Cambridge, abbot 1183-95	Henry II, 1154-1189
John de Cella, 1195-1214	Richard I, 1189-1199 John, 1199-1216
Matthew Paris, historian of St Albans 1199-1259	
William of Trumpington, abbot 1214-1235 1265 death of John of Hertford	Henry III, 1216-1272 Edward I, 1272-1307
1379 death of Adam Rous, surgeon to Edward III 1379 death of Adam Wittenham, cellarer, forester and prior John de la Moote, abbot 1396-1401, last abbot to be buried in the chapter house	Edward II, 1307-1327 Edward III, 1327-1377 Richard II, 1377-1399 Henry IV, 1399-1413 Henry V, 1413-1422 Henry VI, 1422 and finally
1452-92 reconstruction of the chapter house under John of Whethamstede (1452-1465) and William of Wallingford (1476-1492)	deposed 1471 Edward IV, 1461; restored 1471-1483 Edward V, 1483 Richard III, 1483-1485 Henry VII, 1485-1509
1539 Dissolution of the Abbey	Henry VIII, 1509-1547

EXCAVATION
The early fifteenth-century account of the burials in the Chapter House is printed in the original Latin in H.T. Riley (ed.), *Annales Monasterii S.Albani a Johanne Amundesham*, Rolls series, i (London, 1870), pp.434-5. It was translated with notes by Ridgway Lloyd, *An Account of the Altars, Monuments, & Tombs, existing A.D. 1428 in Saint Alban's Abbey* (Saint Albans, 1873), pp. 7-8, from which the translation given by Martin Biddle is adapted.

The account of the grave of Robert of the Chamber is given in H.T. Riley (ed.), *Gesta Abbatum Monasterii Sancti Albani*, Rolls Series, i (London, 1867), p.125.

An account of the excavation in 1978 appears in Martin Biddle and Birthe Kjølbye-Biddle, 'England's Premier Abbey. The Medieval Chapter House of St. Albans Abbey, and its Excavation in 1978', *Expedition*, The University Museum Magazine of Archaeology/Anthropology, University of Pennsylvania, 22.2 (Winter 1980), pp.17-32. This article appears in a revised and slightly expanded version in *Hertfordshire's Past*, 11 (Autumn 1981), pp.3-27.

The final report on the excavation of 1978 by Martin Biddle and Birthe Kjølbye-Biddle, with 36 other contributors, will appear as *The Medieval Chapter House of St Albans Abbey* in the monograph series of *Hertfordshire Archaeology*.

SUCCESSION
The Abbots
Matthew Paris, *Gesta Abbatum Monasterii Sancti Albani*, ed. J. Wats in *Vitae duorum Ofarum ... et viginti trium Abbatum Sancti Albani* (London, 1639) or ed. H.T. Riley in Thomas Walsingham, *Gesta Abbatum monasterii Sancti Albani* 1 (London, Rolls Series, 1867)

R. Vaughan, *Matthew Paris* (Cambridge 1958 and 1980)

L.F.R. Williams, *History of the Abbey of St Albans* (London, 1917)

C.N.L. Brooke, D. Knowles and V. London, *Heads of Religious Houses; England and Wales 940-1216* (Cambridge, 1972)

D. Knowles, *The Monastic Order in England* (Cambridge, 2nd ed. 1963)

The Manuscripts
Rodney M. Thomson, *Manuscripts from St Albans Abbey 1066-1235*, published for the University of Tasmania by D.S. Brewer, (Woodbridge, 1982)

C.R. Dodwell, F. Wormald and O. Pächt, *The St Albans Psalter* (London, 1960)

W. Cahn, 'St Albans and the Channel style in England', in *The Year 1200* (New York, Metropolitan Museum, 1970), pp. 187-211

R.W. Hunt, 'The Library of St Albans Abbey', in *Medieval Scribes, Manuscripts and Libraries; Essays presented to N. R. Ker*, ed. M.B. Parkes and A.G. Watson (London, 1978), pp. 251-77

N.R. Ker, *English Manuscripts in the Century after the Norman Conquest* (Oxford, 1960)

Sir W. Oakeshott, *The Two Winchester Bibles* (Oxford, 1981)

TRADITION
The Rule of St Benedict, edited and translated into English by Justin McCann (London, 1954)

Esther De Waal, *Seeking God: the way of St Benedict* (London, 1984)

C.E. Lawrence, *Medieval Monasticism. Forms of Religious life in Western Europe in the Middle Ages* (London, 2nd ed. 1989)

INSCRIPTION
D. Kindersley & L. Lopes Cardozo, *Letters Slate Cut* (Cambridge, 2nd ed. 1991)

Robert Runcie
Priest, formerly Archbishop of Canterbury and
Primate of all England

Professor Martin Biddle FBA
Astor Senior Research Fellow &
Tutor in Archaeology,
Hertford College Oxford

Birthe Kjølbye-Biddle FSA
Magister. Research Director, Winchester
Research Unit.

Dr Rosamond McKitterick
Historian and palaeographer; Reader in early
mediaeval European history in the University of
Cambridge and Fellow of Newnham College.

Dom Patrick Barry
Abbot of Ampleforth Abbey and lettercutter

David Kindersley
Stonecutter and type designer

Lida Lopes Cardozo
Lettercutter and publisher